A Note to Parents

DK READERS is a compelling program for beginning readers, designed in conjunction with leading literacy experts, including Dr. Linda Gambrell, Distinguished Professor of Education at Clemson University. Dr. Gambrell has served as President of the National Reading Conference, the College Reading Association, and the International Reading Association.

Beautiful illustrations and superb full-color photographs combine with engaging, easy-to-read stories to offer a fresh approach to each subject in the series. Each DK READER is guaranteed to capture a child's interest while developing his or her reading skills, general knowledge, and love of reading.

The five levels of DK READERS are aimed at different reading abilities, enabling you to choose the books that are exactly right for your child:

Pre-level 1: Learning to read
Level 1: Beginning to read
Level 2: Beginning to read alone
Level 3: Reading alone
Level 4: Proficient readers

The "normal" age at which a child begins to read can be anywhere from three to eight years old. Adult participation through the lower levels is very helpful for providing encouragement, discussing storylines, and sounding out unfamiliar words.

No matter which level you select, you can be sure that you are helping your child learn to read, then read to learn!

LONDON, NEW YORK, MUNICH,
MELBOURNE, AND DELHI

For Dorling Kindersley
Senior Editor Laura Gilbert
Design Manager Ron Stobbart
Publishing Manager Catherine Saunders
Art Director Lisa Lanzarini
Publisher Simon Beecroft
Publishing Director Alex Allan
Production Editor Marc Staples
Production Controller Nick Seston
Reading Consultant Dr. Linda Gambrell

For Lucasfilm
Executive Editor J. W. Rinzler
Art Director Troy Alders
Keeper of the Holocron Leland Chee
Director of Publishing Carol Roeder

Designer Sandra Perry
Jacket designed by Jon Hall
Editor Jo Casey

First published in the United States in 2012
by DK Publishing
375 Hudson Street
New York, New York 10014
10 9 8 7 6 5 4 3 2 1
Copyright © 2012 Lucasfilm Ltd and ™
All rights reserved. Used under authorization.
Page design copyright © 2012 Dorling Kindersley Limited
001—182143—Jan/12

Published in Great Britain by Dorling Kindersley Limited

DK books are available at special discounts when purchased in bulk
for sales promotions, premiums, fund-raising, or educational use.
For details, contact:
DK Publishing Special Markets
375 Hudson Street
New York, New York 10014
SpecialSales@dk.com

A catalog record for this book is available
from the Library of Congress.

ISBN: 978-0-7566-8866-0 (Paperback)
ISBN: 978-0-7566-8865-3 (Hardcover)

Color reproduction by Media Development and Printing, UK
Printed and bound in China by L. Rex Printing Co., Ltd

Discover more at
www.dk.com
www.starwars.com

Contents

DK READERS

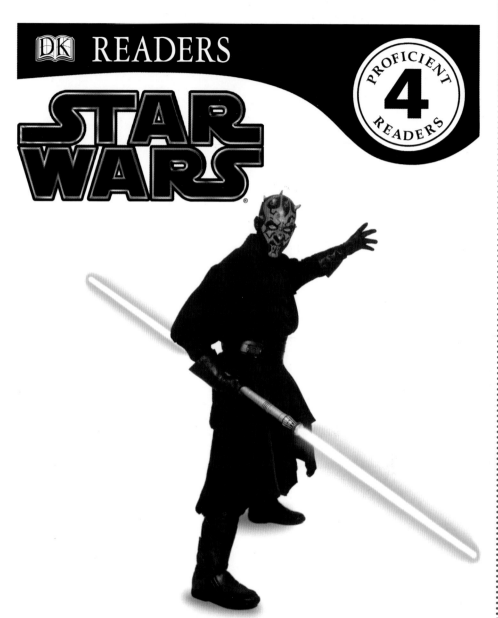

STAR WARS

PROFICIENT 4 READERS

DARTH MAUL

SITH APPRENTICE

Written by Jo Casey and Catherine Saunders

Ancient Order
The Sith Order
was formed
thousands of
years ago by a
Jedi who had
turned to the
dark side of
the Force.

The Force
The Force is a
type of energy
created by all
living things.
It has two
sides—a light
side (good) and
a dark side (bad).

The Sith

Beware! Evil is lurking.
The mysterious Order called the
Sith is secretly plotting to take
over the galaxy. The Sith use the
dark side of the Force to gain great
power. They draw their strength
from strong emotions such as
anger, passion, and fear.

The Jedi are the enemies of the
Sith. They believed that they had
destroyed all the Sith 1,000 years
ago. But the Order survived
and the Sith continued in
hiding. The Sith also
introduced the Rule of Two,
which means that there can
only ever be two Sith at one
time—a Master and an apprentice.
When the time comes, the
apprentice will defeat his Master
and take his place. He will then
take on a new apprentice and
continue the evil work of the Sith.

For many years the galaxy has been at peace, ruled by a democratic Senate. But Sith Master Darth Sidious and his apprentice Darth Maul have been waiting patiently in the shadows. Finally, it is time to reveal their existence and put their evil plan into action. They will face their old enemy, the Jedi, again.

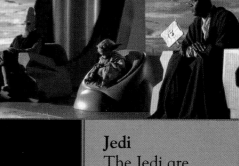

Jedi
The Jedi are peacekeepers of the galaxy. They use the light side of the Force to promote justice and peace.

Secret apprentice
Sith apprentice Darth Maul is the first Sith to reveal himself for 1,000 years.

Return of the Sith

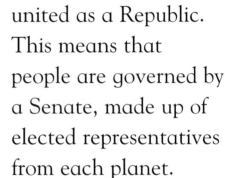

While the Sith have been in hiding, the galaxy has been united as a Republic. This means that people are governed by a Senate, made up of elected representatives from each planet.

Senator Palpatine
Palpatine is the planet of Naboo's trusted representative in the Senate. He is a well-respected Senator.

The Trade Federation
The Trade Federation is the largest trading corporation in the galaxy. It is controlled by greedy Neimoidians.

The Sith think it is time to change this—the galaxy should be ruled by them instead! So, the Sith begin to secretly manipulate events.

When the Senate decides to tax trade routes, the Trade Federation fears it will lose profit. Encouraged by Darth Sidious, the Trade Federation creates a battleship blockade around the peaceful planet of Naboo. This could mean war!

However, Naboo's leader, Queen Amidala, would rather settle the dispute peacefully. She seeks advice from Naboo's Senator Palpatine.

To help Amidala, Palpatine speaks to the leader of the Senate, Supreme Chancellor Valorum. The Chancellor sends the Jedi Qui-Gon Jinn and Obi-Wan Kenobi to meet the Trade Federation and seek a peaceful solution to the conflict. But Darth Sidious doesn't want peace, so the Trade Federation will not negotiate!

The Galactic Senate is where representatives from the planets of the Republic gather to make important decisions.

Queen Amidala
Amidala was elected Queen of Naboo when she was 14 years old. She lives in a palace in Naboo's capital, Theed.

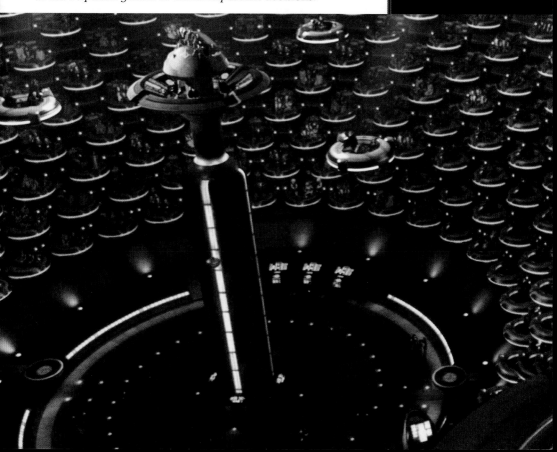

Greedy Neimoidians
Nute Gunray is Viceroy of the Trade Federation. He cares only about making money and will work with anyone that will make him a profit.

Dark plan

Darth Sidious orders the Neimoidians to have Qui-Gon Jinn and Obi-Wan Kenobi destroyed as soon as they arrive on the Trade Federation's battleship. But the Jedi are not so easy to attack.

The Jedi escape to the surface of the planet Naboo. Unfortunately, the Trade Federation and its droid army are about to invade Naboo and take Queen Amidala hostage! Luckily, the two Jedi rescue Queen Amidala and agree to help her save Naboo.

Qui-Gon, Obi-Wan, and Amidala set off for the Senate to plead for help. But their ship is damaged by the cannons of the blockade and they are forced to land on the planet Tatooine for repairs.

Darth Sidious will not let these Jedi ruin his evil plans to take over the galaxy. He knows just who to send to locate and stop them—his apprentice Darth Maul. Maul is ready to face the Jedi. They will be no match for a deadly Sith like him!

Escape
The Jedi and Amidala escape in the Queen's Royal Starship.

Shadowy Sith
Darth Sidious gives his orders via hologram. Darth Maul is a silent, yet menacing, presence behind him.

Senator Palpatine

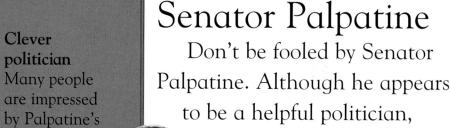

Clever politician
Many people are impressed by Palpatine's decisive approach to politics.

Don't be fooled by Senator Palpatine. Although he appears to be a helpful politician, underneath his friendly exterior he is hiding a very dark secret.

When Queen Amidala eventually arrives at the Senate to ask for help for Naboo, Senator Palpatine is right by her side. The Senate, however, appears reluctant to help.

So Palpatine persuades Amidala that Supreme Chancellor Valorum is weak and that a new Chancellor is needed. This is all part of Palpatine's secret plan: He convinces the Senate to vote for a new Supreme Chancellor—himself!

As Supreme Chancellor, Palpatine promises to end corruption and bring order to the galaxy. The planet of Naboo is sure to be safe with Palpatine as Supreme Chancellor—isn't it?

Now that Supreme Chancellor Palpatine is the most powerful person in the Senate, he can put the next stage of his secret plan into action. Will anyone be able to stop him before it is too late?

Deadly Sith
Darth Sidious plans to destroy the Republic and gain supreme power over the galaxy.

Sith Master

Meet Darth Sidious—the most powerful Sith Master who has ever lived. Now take a closer look. Does his face look a little familiar? It is actually Chancellor Palpatine. Darth Sidious's dark side powers are so strong that no one suspects that the Supreme Chancellor is also an evil Sith Lord!

Almost no one knows
that Darth Sidious even
exists, let alone what he
looks like. He always wears
a hooded black cloak, which
conceals his face. When he gives
orders to the Trade Federation he
does so via hologram so that he
never reveals his true identity or his
exact location.

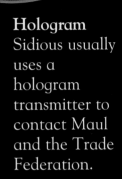

Hologram
Sidious usually
uses a
hologram
transmitter to
contact Maul
and the Trade
Federation.

In accordance with the Rule of
Two, Sidious defeated
Sith Master Darth
Plagueis and took his
place. Sidious then
chose his own
apprentice, Darth
Maul. Maul is a
ruthless assassin,
trained to follow his
Master's orders.

*Sith use anger and rage
in battle, making them
ferocious foes to face.*

Darth Maul

Darth Sidious's apprentice is deadly, strong, ferocious—and dedicated to the dark side.

Darth Sidious first discovered Maul's Force-potential when Maul was an infant. Given to him by a Nightsister, Sidious immediately began raising him to someday become his apprentice.

Sidious's training methods were often harsh and unforgiving, but as a result Darth Maul is now a powerful and completely relentless fighter.

Maul is an obedient apprentice and he obeys his Master without question. Nothing scares him, not even the thought of fighting two Jedi.

Fearsome foe
Darth Maul is a Zabrak from the planet Dathomir. His weapon is a double-bladed lightsaber.

Maul often communicates with his Master via hologram.

It is Maul who finally reveals
the existence of the Sith to
the Jedi when he tracks
them down on Tatooine.
His Master will remain hidden
until the time is right.

Sith powers
Darth Maul
uses powerful
emotions, such
as anger and
hatred, to gain
strength from
the dark side.

Horns

Double-bladed
lightsaber

Black hooded
robe

Yellow eyes

Black tattoos

Origins
Before he was
taken in by
Sidious, Maul
was destined
to become
a member
of a warrior
tribe called the
Nightbrothers of
Dathomir. The
Nightbrothers
were ruled
by the female
Nightsisters
clan.

Black leather
combat gloves

Heavy
action
boots

Zabrak warrior

Darth Maul looks terrifying, even for a Sith. His unique appearance reflects not only his allegiance to the dark side, but also reveals his origins.

Maul is a Zabrak and was born on the planet Dathomir, home to the Nightbrothers and his brother Savage Opress. Zabraks are similar to humans in many ways, but they have a few differences. Zabraks can have many colored skin tones, including red, yellow, brown, and black. Zabraks also have horns on their heads and distinctive facial tattoos. These tattoos can symbolize family loyalty and place of birth, or can reflect the personality of the individual Zabrak.

Maul's yellow eyes show that he is a powerful Sith and devoted to the dark side of the Force.

Horns
A Zabrak's horns appear early in life and can grow in varying numbers and patterns on their heads.

Not human
Zabraks have some similar facial features to humans, but they cannot grow eyelashes or facial hair.

17

Sith technology

Maul's Force powers are strong, but even this deadly Sith needs some specialist equipment to help him track down the Jedi and Queen Amidala. Using his powerful Infiltrator ship, Maul follows them to Tatooine.

Maul's Infiltrator was given to him by his Master, Darth Sidious, and Maul named it the *Scimitar*. The ship has a round cockpit and a pair of folding wings. It also has an invisibility field generator, which helps Maul and his ship to avoid detection and capture. The Sith finds this device very useful!

Invisible ship
The invisibility field generator in the *Scimitar* is powered by stygium crystals, found on the planet of Aeten II in the Outer Rim.

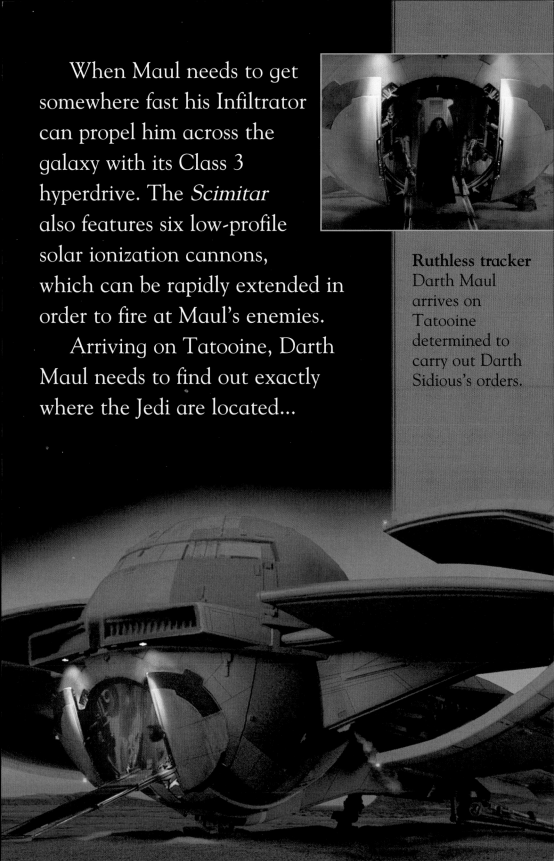

When Maul needs to get somewhere fast his Infiltrator can propel him across the galaxy with its Class 3 hyperdrive. The *Scimitar* also features six low-profile solar ionization cannons, which can be rapidly extended in order to fire at Maul's enemies.

Arriving on Tatooine, Darth Maul needs to find out exactly where the Jedi are located...

Ruthless tracker Darth Maul arrives on Tatooine determined to carry out Darth Sidious's orders.

Weapon
Maul's electrobinoculars can also be attached to blasters so that he can attack his enemies from long range.

Controls

Electronic lens

Grip

Powerful tool
Maul can use the electrobinoculars to view targets in most weather conditions. They also have a useful night vision mode.

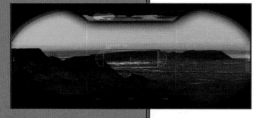

Darth Maul's *Scimitar* also features various compartments. These contain useful equipment including three DRK-1 probe droids, a speeder bike, several interrogation and security droids, torture devices, spying equipment, bombs, and mines. Arriving on Tatooine undetected, thanks to his ship's invisibility field generator, Maul now needs to find out exactly where the Jedi are—without revealing his own existence. The Sith's electrobinoculars enable him to locate the Jedi's ship and observe the craft from afar. This powerful gadget is able to magnify distant objects so that Darth Maul can study his prey far more closely.

An inbuilt computer system calculates the coordinates of his target and can record up to three hours worth of images. Maul has gathered some useful information. However, it is not yet time to reveal his presence to his enemy.

Far and wide Maul's enemies have no place to hide from his all-seeing electrobinoculars.

Probe droids are best suited to tracking on a planet's surface, rather than in space.

Silent spies
Qui-Gon Jinn has no idea that a probe droid, sent by Maul, is spying on him.

The Sith have been in hiding for a long time and Darth Maul is determined not to make a move against the Jedi and Amidala until the right moment. The Sith has located the Royal Starship on Tatooine, but he needs to discover the exact location of his enemies. So Maul sends three probe droids to gather this information.

The tiny but powerful DRK-1 or "Dark Eye" droids are controlled via Maul's wristlink. They contain image sensors that can send important data back to Maul and are designed to pass through crowds silently and largely unnoticed.

One of the droids finally locates Qui-Gon and reports back to Maul. The Sith is ready to begin his deadly mission!

Small but deadly
Dark Eye probe droids can also be fitted with small, powerful weapons such as blasters.

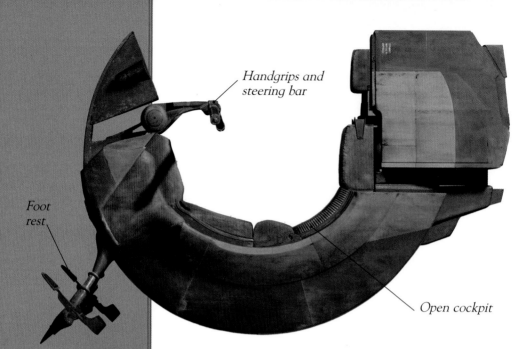

Handgrips and steering bar

Foot rest

Open cockpit

Combat ready
The open cockpit of the *Bloodfin* allows Maul to leap into combat directly from his speeder.

Ready to battle
As soon as Maul locates his enemies on Tatooine, he jumps onto his speeder bike to find them.

Darth Maul possesses the ideal vehicle for crossing the deserts of Tatooine. His sleek speeder bike can reach speeds of 650 km/h (404 mph) in seconds. It is a modified Razalon FC-20 speeder bike and is named after a vicious aquatic creature Maul once fought in the Outer Rim territories—the Bloodfin.

Bloodfin is a small, compact bike, powered by a repulsorlift engine. This powerful anti-gravity engine enables the rider to accelerate rapidly and turn corners sharply.

Maul can even pilot the vehicle remotely using either his Force powers or his wristlink. An auto brake also means that when Maul leaps into battle, his speeder stops automatically. The main purpose of the *Bloodfin* is pursuit, rather than attack, so it is not equipped with any weapons. Maul himself is deadly enough—as the Jedi are just about to find out...

Silent attacker
As Maul approaches on his speeder, young Anakin Skywalker is unaware of him.

Sith attack!

The moment that Darth Maul has been waiting for has come at last. He is about to test his skills in a battle against the Sith's greatest enemy—the Jedi.

While waiting for his ship to be repaired on Tatooine, Jedi Master Qui-Gon Jinn senses a disturbance in the Force. Something is wrong, but what can it mean? Suddenly, a cloaked figure on a speeder bike appears in the distance.

Bad feeling
Jedi and Sith are attuned to the Force and can often sense when the balance is disturbed.

Tatooine
Tatooine is a desert planet located in the Outer Rim of the galaxy.

Darth Maul has been training for this moment all his life. He is a formidable opponent, but so is Qui-Gon. The Jedi and Sith fight a short duel until Obi-Wan Kenobi arrives with the repaired starship. Qui-Gon uses a Force jump to board the ship and escapes. The battle is over—for now. This attack can mean only one thing: The Sith are back!

Skilled Jedi
Qui-Gon has never had to duel a Sith before and his lightsaber skills are put to the test.

Old enemy
Qui-Gon feels sure that his attacker was a Sith. This is troubling news for the Jedi— and the galaxy!

The Jedi Order

Headquarters
The Jedi Council meet in the Jedi Temple, on the planet of Coruscant. The Galactic Senate is also located on Coruscant.

Now that the Sith have revealed their existence, Qui-Gon Jinn and Obi-Wan Kenobi need to break the bad news to their fellow Jedi. If the Sith are back, difficult times are sure to follow.

The Jedi are guided by the Jedi High Council. It is here that decisions are made about who should become a Jedi and how the Jedi should act. The Council is made up of 12 of the most powerful Jedi.

Members are selected for their
skills such as wisdom, foresight,
and intuition. The most senior
Council members are Mace
Windu, Ki-Adi Mundi, and
Grand Master Yoda.

At first even these great Jedi
cannot believe that their old
enemies are back. How could the
Sith have returned without the
Jedi sensing their presence?
The Jedi resolve to unravel
this strange mystery.

Yoda
Grand Master
Yoda is the
leader of the
Jedi High
Council. He is
900 years old
and extremely
powerful.

29

Jedi strengths

The Jedi Order is respected for its wisdom and honor. The Jedi use the light side of the Force to promote peace and justice throughout the galaxy. Despite their Force powers, however, the Jedi could not foresee the return of the Sith. Now the Jedi will need all their strength to face the threat of the dark side.

Although the Jedi and Sith are enemies, they share some similarities. Both gain power through studying the Force and both believe in the importance of the Master and apprentice relationship.

Skilled Master Qui-Gon is a wise and experienced Jedi Master.

The Jedi do not follow the Rule of Two—there can be as many Jedi as can prove themselves worthy of the name.

But a Jedi Master acts very differently from a Sith Master. A Jedi Master trains his apprentice, called a Padawan, with patience. He passes on his own skills and hopes that one day his Padawan will become a Jedi Knight and then a Jedi Master. The Jedi Master and Padawan relationship is based on loyalty and respect, not fear.

Teamwork
Unlike the Sith, a Jedi Master and his Padawan usually go on missions together.

Both a Sith apprentice and a Jedi apprentice begin their training at a young age. If Force potential is discovered in them, they are taken away from their family to begin training. Jedi Younglings study the basics of the light side of the Force as a group. The best Younglings then become Padawans. A young Sith, however, spends much of his time alone and is taught by a fearsome Master.

Younglings
Younglings wear a special training helmet which covers their eyes. This helps them learn to "see" only by using the Force.

Friends
Padawan and Master often develop a close and loyal bond.

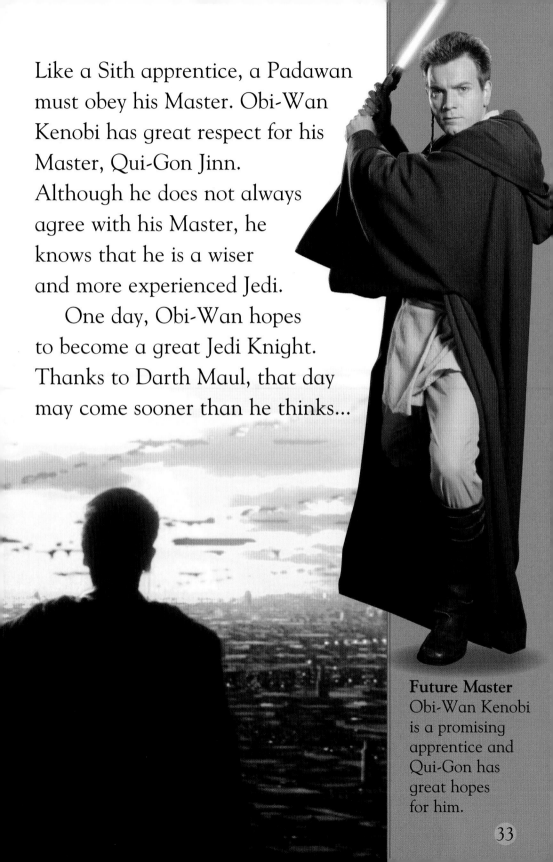

Like a Sith apprentice, a Padawan must obey his Master. Obi-Wan Kenobi has great respect for his Master, Qui-Gon Jinn. Although he does not always agree with his Master, he knows that he is a wiser and more experienced Jedi.

One day, Obi-Wan hopes to become a great Jedi Knight. Thanks to Darth Maul, that day may come sooner than he thinks...

Future Master
Obi-Wan Kenobi is a promising apprentice and Qui-Gon has great hopes for him.

Master and apprentice
Sith Master Darth Sidious and his apprentice Darth Maul are determined to bring the galaxy under the rule of the Sith.

The Rule of Two

While the Jedi seek peace and harmony, the Sith start wars and harness the power of anger and fear. Many years ago there were lots of Sith. But their allegiance to the dark side meant that they were concerned only with their own interests and often disagreed with each other. As a result, the Sith nearly destroyed themselves. The Rule of Two was introduced to limit their number and prevent the power of the dark side destroying the Order.

In many ways, Darth Maul is the perfect Sith apprentice—obedient, powerful, and ruthless. Sidious has trained him well and is pleased with him. But their thirst for power dictates that when the time is right, Maul must overthrow his Master. There is no loyalty among the Sith, only fear and suspicion.

Rival
One day Maul will challenge his Master. This means that Sidious must be watchful of his apprentice at all times.

For now, Maul follows Sidious's orders without question.

Deadly lightsaber

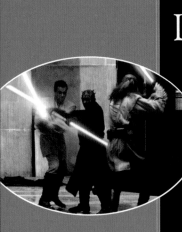

Red blades
The Jedi mostly favor blue and green lightsaber blades, built using natural crystals. However, the Sith prefer red blades, which are made from artificial crystals.

Two into one
Darth Maul created his unique lightsaber by welding two separate lightsabers together.

Although the Sith and Jedi use the Force in very different ways, they share a common weapon—the lightsaber. This ancient sword is very powerful, particularly when wielded by someone with Force powers. Each Sith or Jedi builds their own lightsaber, so each one may suit the owner's individual style and taste. At the heart of every lightsaber is an energy crystal that gives the sword's blade its bright color.

Darth Maul's chosen weapon is a double-bladed lightsaber, which is also known as a saberstaff. Its design is based on an ancient Zabrak weapon called a Zhaboka. The twin blades make it twice as deadly as the single-bladed lightsabers used by the Jedi. This also means that Maul can take on two opponents at once.

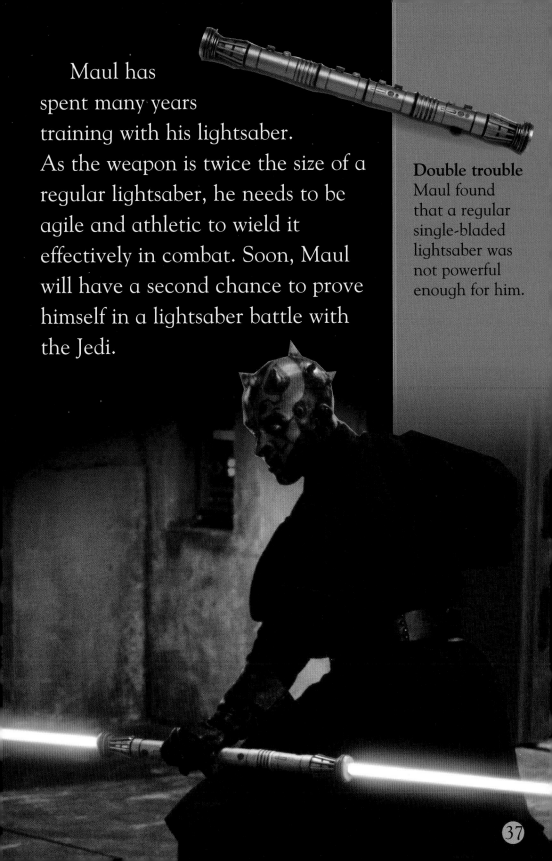

Maul has spent many years training with his lightsaber. As the weapon is twice the size of a regular lightsaber, he needs to be agile and athletic to wield it effectively in combat. Soon, Maul will have a second chance to prove himself in a lightsaber battle with the Jedi.

Double trouble Maul found that a regular single-bladed lightsaber was not powerful enough for him.

Allies
Amidala needs
help to defend
Naboo so she
forms an
alliance with
the Gungans,
who also live
on the planet.

Darth Maul
The Sith
apprentice has
been waiting
for another
opportunity to
attack the Jedi.

The Battle for Naboo

After meeting with the Senate in
Coruscant, Queen Amidala realizes
that the time for negotiation has
passed. She decides that she must
return home to Naboo and defend
her planet.

The Jedi can fight when
necessary, so they go with Amidala
to Naboo. Jedi Master Mace Windu
also believes that this mission may
provide an opportunity to discover
more about the mysterious warrior
who attacked Qui-Gon on Tatooine.

Queen Amidala formulates a clever plan that just might work: While the Gungans keep the battle droids busy, Amidala and the Jedi head to Theed to liberate Naboo's capital and capture Nute Gunray. They also free Naboo's pilots who have been held hostage. The pilots quickly leap into action and launch an attack on the Droid Control Ship. Things are looking good for Naboo. But the Sith haven't given up just yet...

Control Ship
The Trade Federation's army is made up of thousands of battle droids. They are controlled via a battleship that orbits Naboo.

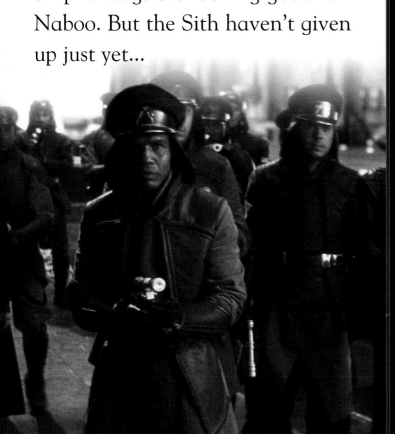

Droid army
If the Naboo pilots can destroy the control ship, the battle droids will be shut down.

Round two

Sidious is closely watching the battle unfold on Naboo: Conflict is good for the Sith— it creates uncertainty, fear, and destruction. Power is within the Sith Master's grasp! Sidious sends his apprentice to Naboo to finish what he started on Tatooine. This time Darth Maul will not fail.

New threat
Maul suddenly appears in the midst of the battle for control of Naboo.

Two against one
On Tatooine, Maul fought Qui-Gon. This time he must battle Obi-Wan as well.

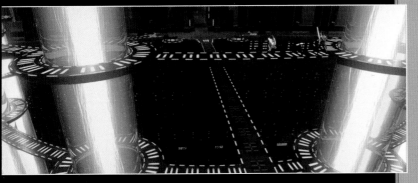

Theed Power Generator
The generator is a source of plasmic energy that powers Naboo.

When Maul arrives on Naboo, Qui-Gon and Obi-Wan take him on, while Amidala sneaks into Theed palace to overthrow the Neimoidians. Maul leads the Jedi toward the Theed Power Generator, a huge, dangerous maze of high platforms and deep shafts. This time Maul must test his skills against two powerful Jedi. The deadly Sith is still confident he can defeat them both and, sure enough, he soon separates Obi-Wan from his Master.

Sith advantage
Maul pushes Obi-Wan out of the way so that he can fight Qui-Gon alone.

Helpless
Obi-Wan is
separated from
his Master
behind the
electron ray
doors and can
do nothing to
help his Master.

Power
Qui-Gon
meditates,
waiting for the
doors to re-open.

Apprentice vs. apprentice

While Obi-Wan watches helplessly, Qui-Gon continues to battle Darth Maul. The Jedi and Sith battle fiercely, but the Sith proves to be a superior fighter and deals Qui-Gon a fatal blow. Obi-Wan must now battle Maul, alone. But first the young Padawan needs to control his feelings of anger and grief. He must gain strength and courage from the light side of the Force.

Obi-Wan is a great fighter and slices the Sith's lightsaber in two. But Maul manages to recover quickly.

He uses the Force to push Obi-Wan over the edge of the generator's core. Maul then kicks the Jedi's lightsaber into the abyss, leaving him defenseless. As Obi-Wan dangles over the edge of the bottomless core, it seems as though the Sith apprentice has finally won.

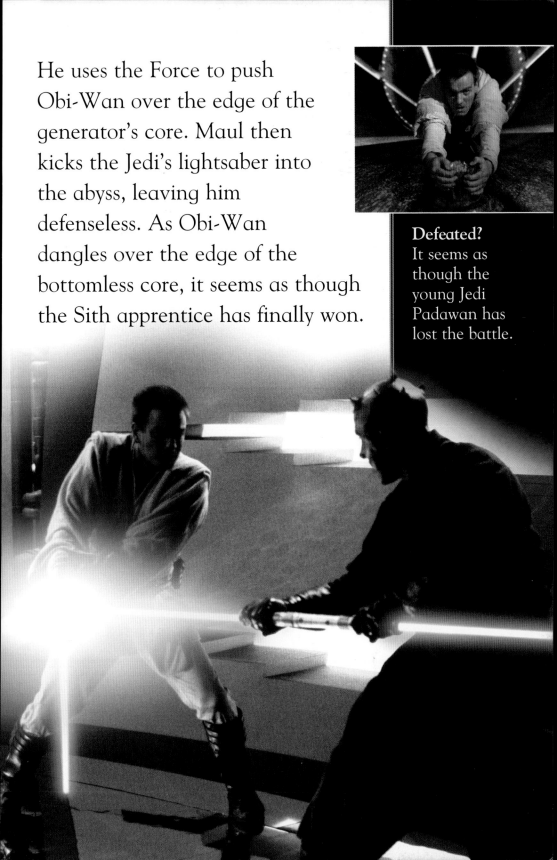

Defeated?
It seems as though the young Jedi Padawan has lost the battle.

The end of Maul

Maul is confident that he has beaten the Jedi. But the Sith has fatally underestimated the Jedi. Obi-Wan senses Qui-Gon's lightsaber and summons up all his Force powers to vault back to the top of the shaft and grab it.

With one deadly blow of his Master's lightsaber, Obi-Wan defeats Darth Maul and sends his nearly lifeless body spinning down the reactor core. Obi-Wan has won the duel!

On this occasion, the light side of the Force has triumphed over the dark side, although a great Jedi Master has sacrificed his life in the process. Amidala and the people of Naboo are also victorious. Maul is defeated and Sidious's plan to take over the galaxy has failed—for now.

The Sith return
Darth Maul's second appearance on Naboo has confirmed that the Sith truly are back!

Celebration
Amidala's plan worked! The Trade Federation is defeated and the people of Naboo liberated.

A new apprentice

The death of Darth Maul means that Darth Sidious must take on a new apprentice. Even the powerful Sith Master cannot carry out his evil plan to take over the galaxy without some help.

Jedi Master
Many years ago, Qui-Gon Jinn was Dooku's Padawan.

This time, however, Darth Sidious does not have time to train a young apprentice. His desire for power is as strong as ever, despite the setbacks he has suffered on Naboo. So, Sidious selects former Jedi Master Count Dooku, and trains him in the dark side of the Force.

As a former Jedi, Dooku already has many useful skills.

Dooku is a very different kind of apprentice from Darth Maul. He has his own ideas and plans.

Dooku had been a brave and respected member of the Jedi, but grew frustrated with the limitations of the Order. Dooku eventually left, becoming one of only 20 members who have ever left the Jedi Order.

Senator Palpatine had sensed Dooku's negative feelings for many years and after the death of Darth Maul, seized the opportunity to convince him to become his new Sith apprentice. It was not difficult.

Together, Dooku and Sidious are determined to gain control of the galaxy. Dark times lie ahead...

Future apprentice? Chancellor Palpatine also seems very interested in the career of a young Jedi Anakin Skywalker...

Glossary

Agile
Quick and well-coordinated.

Allegiance
Dedication or commitment to a person, group, or cause.

Apprentice
A trainee or learner.

Assassin
A murderer of an important person, usually for political or religious reasons.

Corruption
Dishonest behavior by those in power.

Dark side
The part of the Force associated with fear and hatred.

Decisive
The ability to make decisions quickly.

Devious
Dishonest and sly.

Droid
A kind of robot.

Exterior
The outward behavior or appearance of a person.

Force
The energy created by all living things.

Galaxy
A group of millions of stars and planets.

Jedi Council
The governing body of the Jedi Order. The wisest Jedi, such as Yoda, sit on the Council.

Jedi Knight
A warrior with special powers who defends the good of the galaxy.

Jedi Master
The most experienced Jedi of all.

Jedi Order
The name of a group that defends peace and justice in the galaxy.

Light side
The part of the Force associated with goodness, compassion, and healing.

Loyalty
Being devoted to something or someone.

Manipulate
To influence by unfair means, especially to one's own advantage.

Missions
Special tasks or duties.

Opponents
People who fight against each other in a duel.

Padawan Learner
A Jedi who is learning the ways of the Force.

Republic
A nation or group of nations in which the people vote for their leaders.

Revenge
To inflict punishment in return for an insult or injury.

Senate
The governing body of the Republic.

Senator
A member of the Senate. He or she will have been chosen (elected) by the people of his or her country.

Superior
A person or thing that is higher in rank, status, or quality.

Underestimates
Doesn't value someone's abilities highly enough.

Wield
To handle a weapon or tool with ease.

Youngling
The first stage of Jedi training, before you become a Padawan Learner.

Index

DK READERS

PROFICIENT 4 READERS

Get ready to enter the dark side and discover everything about the evil Darth Maul—if you dare!

DK READERS

Stunning photographs combine with lively illustrations and engaging, age-appropriate stories in DK READERS, a multilevel reading program guaranteed to capture children's interest while developing their reading skills and general knowledge.

	Level	Features
LEARNING 1 pre-level TO READ	Learning to read	• High-frequency words • Picture word strips, picture glossary, and simple index • Labels to introduce and reinforce vocabulary • High level of adult participation helpful
BEGINNING 1 TO READ	Beginning to read	• Simple sentences and limited vocabulary • Picture glossary and simple index • Adult participation helpful
BEGINNING 2 TO READ ALONE	Beginning to read alone	• Longer sentences and increased vocabulary • Information boxes full of extra fun facts • Simple index • Occasional adult participation helpful
READING 3 ALONE	Reading alone	• More complex sentence structure • Information boxes and alphabetical glossary • Comprehensive index
PROFICIENT 4 READERS	Proficient readers	• Rich vocabulary and challenging sentence structure • Additional information and alphabetical glossary • Comprehensive index

With DK READERS, children will learn to read—then read to learn!

Printed in China

LUCAS BOOKS

Visit the official website: **starwars.com**

© 2012 Lucasfilm Ltd. and TM.
All Rights Reserved.
Used Under Authorization.

$3.99 USA
$4.99 Canada

Discover more at
www.dk.com

ISBN 978-0-7566-8866-0

50399

9 780756 688660